When in doubt

Applying the programmer's debugging
mindset to your everyday life

–

Émile Perron

Contents

Preface

If a simple change of mindset could help you improve the quality of your relationships, your work and your day-to-day life... Would you be willing to try it?

If you said yes, then you're in luck, because that is precisely what I will be telling you about in this book.

Before we get started, I would like to introduce myself in order to give you some context about where the main principle behind this book comes from. My name is Émile, and I am a web developer. I have been playing around with computers since the early 2000s; my parents and relatives often like to mention the fact that I could browse the Internet by myself before I learned to read or write. Therefore, it is no wonder that early in my childhood, I got interested in programming and started learning everything I could about the subject.

Don't let me fool you: I was not an expert or a prodigy by any stretch of the imagination. To this day, I still consider myself to be at the same skill level as your average developer. I did, however, do well enough to create websites and programs on my own, starting in primary school. This helped me quite a bit in high school and college, because as it turns out, you could build programs on the TI-83 Plus calculators that were required to attend most math and science classes. As you might have guessed, I used that to my advantage by creating programs in which I could simply input the information from the question prompt and get the answers I needed in return. With a little skill and creativity, you could also create games on those calculators – that is what I ended up doing during most of my classes.

Once I was done with college, I started working in a small web and design agency, where I still work to this day, over 4 years later. I have also worked on many personal projects, some of which proved to be useful and remain up and running to this day, while others have been terminated for lack of interest, usefulness or popularity.

The point that I am trying to get across with this introduction is that I am not a seasoned and successful entrepreneur or a top dog working in a well-known tech company. However, I truly believe that the principle that this book is about can help you in most aspects of your life, and that therefore, you will find more than enough value in the pages to come to justify the time and money you spend on them. This is based on both my personal experience, and the experience of people I know who also apply this mindset.

Obviously, this book will not make you instantly successful, rich or popular. What I will be sharing with you is not magic or wizardry. However, the principle you will find in this book, if applied correctly, may help you improve your relationships. It may help you get that raise that you are hoping for. It may help you increase your quality of life on a day to day basis - not by giving you more money, popularity or material goods, but solely by changing the way you think and react to the events that happen around you.

You do not have to know anything about programming or technologies in general to apply what I will be sharing with you in the upcoming pages. I simply extracted a thought process that I use on a daily basis when I am programming, and found that it could be applied to improve my daily activities. It is incredibly simple and helpful, and yet quite unintuitive.

Have I piqued your curiosity yet? Good, then let us get started.

P.S.

This book will not relate tales of a great Tolkien-like universe, nor will it make you explore mind bending concepts like the works of Jules Verne or Lewis Carroll would. Although the writings to come are not as witty and clever as those of Matt Haig, they also won't be as complex of a read as Thoreau's work can be to most. I am a simple man who likes to write simple things. I hope you will appreciate and learn from the message I am trying to communicate with this book.

Chapter 1

The Basic Principle

Over thousands of years, the human race has evolved to be the most powerful species on Earth. We have spread our kind across the entire globe and developed incredible tools that allow us to communicate with one another. Those tools ensure that we remain the supreme leaders of this planet.

Now, however grandiose that might sound, most of us are actually quite simple beings: we work to get enough money to live, save a little to allow ourselves to take a break towards the end of our lives, and we try to enjoy the ride on our way there. We are creatures of habit, and just like many species, we look for the path of least resistance. After all, it is what many species have evolved to do: get the most "reward" while spending as little time, effort and energy as possible. We do the same, except we often value our efforts and energy much more than we do our time. There is nothing wrong with that, it is simply something we have evolved to do, and it allows us to live in a society that functions fairly well.

Nevertheless, the path of least resistance can sometimes be misleading. It is often the case for programmers such as myself: you have a task to accomplish, you write some code, and then it turns out that the code you wrote doesn't produce the expected result. You take a quick glance at your code, and everything looks right, so obviously the person who built the system you are working with must have made a mistake. Right?

Of course, this initial reaction is usually wrong, but it is very common nonetheless - much more common than you might expect. Yes, it might be the easiest explanation for your problem, as it does not require you to alter your code or to put in any more work, but that does not mean it is right. Even if you are using other people's code inside your program, there is a good chance that the code **you** wrote is to blame. When your program fails, you are most likely the one at fault; it is as simple as that.

Assuming you're wrong

Now, I know you are not reading this book to learn about the human species and how it evolved, nor are you reading it in order to learn about how the debugging process works for programmers and developers. What you most likely want to know is the basic principle behind this entire book, the simple thought process that you can apply in your own life. Here it is:

"When in doubt, assume you're wrong."

Now, let me unpack this for you. At first glance, this might seem to be a very pessimistic way to look at things. After all, when you first read this sentence, it does seem to say that you are the one at fault, at all times. However, that is quite far from the truth and from the message it is meant to convey.

As you are already very well aware, you are not wrong at all times. In fact, most of the decisions that we humans take are fairly good; our instincts, experience and education usually guide us in the right direction. However, when we do make a bad decision, we have a tendency to look for excuses or culprits. As soon as something is wrong, annoying or does not work as intended, most people will simply ignore the problem, blame it on someone else or find a way to make others look past it. The main reason we do this is quite easy to grasp: denying responsibility in such a way often seems to be the easiest solution – the path of least resistance – which, as we pointed out earlier, is what we have evolved to look for. It is rather easy to say that someone else is at fault, and that there is nothing you can do about it. Or even better: that someone else is at fault, and that it is their job to resolve the problem, not yours. However, just like in the programmer's debugging process, you have to start by considering one very important thing: it is highly likely that you are the one who messed up, not someone else.

Say you're at the grocery store, checking out. You hand the cashier a bill, she hands you back your change and says "Thank you, have a nice day!". You look at the amount of money she handed back to you, and it's wrong: you're missing a tenner. So, you tell the cashier she made a mistake. She looks at the screen and says "No, this is right.". You insist, saying you're missing ten dollars, and now the both of you are getting just a tiny bit annoyed by the situation. You then open your wallet, only to realize you handed her the wrong bill. As it turns out, the change she gave you back was right all along.

Now, the error in this scenario might seem inconsequential, but most of us make those types of mistakes all the time, in every aspect of our life. The consequences can be much more important if you make that mistake at work, for example. You wouldn't want to risk losing a big client or to get on the wrong side of your colleague or your boss, just because you didn't handle your own mistakes correctly. Additionally, there are often more people affected by these types of situations than what we originally think about. In the previous scenario, the one with the cashier, you were probably annoyed for a moment, and then you might have felt embarrassed. The cashier might have been annoyed for a moment, because you blamed her for a mistake she didn't make. These two we already knew about. However, there were most likely people in queue behind you, and they might also have gotten annoyed because you ended up delaying them for absolutely nothing. All of that could have been avoided by simply checking your wallet to make sure you hadn't made a mistake yourself before accusing others of having made one. As basic and obvious as this may seem, there is a lot of insight to be gathered from a simple example like this, and you can make use of that insight in many other parts of your life.

The first step in any personal problem-solving case should almost always be to reflect on the part you played in it. Is it possible that you are the one at fault? If so, what is it that you could have done wrong? Only when you have thought about all of the different mistakes you might have made to get to where you are should you begin to think about what others might have done wrong. Allow me to rephrase that sentence so you can read it in a single breath: when in doubt, assume you're wrong.

Figuring things out

As soon as you are implicated in a situation that is problematic in some way, shape or form, your own doings and your own point of view are the most important thing to focus on. After all, the things that you do and see with your own eyes are the only things you can be completely certain about. Your own point of view is all you have to rely on, and therefore most of your reflection should be based on that and that only. Only once you have studied every decision and possibility within your own point of view and within your own doings should you even start to venture into what others might have done.

If you are well-learned in the fields of science or philosophy, you might know this concept of only using data that came from your own experiences as empiricism. This concept is said to be at the root of the scientific method, as it is essential that scientific theories be tested and experienced for yourself instead of simply theorized. It's also at the root of who we are as people: your own experiences, from the first time your consciousness arises in the womb up to this very moment, are what shaped you into the person you are today. What you are told and taught also has an impact, undoubtably, but it's nowhere near as major as the data you gather for yourself using your own senses. Just think about when you were a kid. Even if your parents told you over and over again that eating an entire pack of cookies would make you feel like crap, you just went ahead and did it anyway, right? You munched away on as many cookies as you could get your hands on, only to realize half an hour later that your tummy ached, and that your parents were right. The same thing goes for cacao powder: even if you're told countless times that it's not nearly as tasty and wonderful as chocolate, you don't really know for sure until you grab a spoonful and have it turn into a bitter paste in your mouth. And then you never do it again. That experience stays with you, either consciously or unconsciously, and you grow from it. And that is why relying on your own knowledge and experience is an important first step when you are trying to figure things out. Make use of those experiences, both ancient and recent. Reflect on them, and try to see if they can help you in your current situation.

In many cases, this initial study of your own thoughts and actions will either reveal a solution to your problem or your question, or it will guide you towards what caused a problem or a reflection in the first place, which is the first step to figuring out the former. In all remaining cases, i.e. situations in which you truly cannot find the flaw in your own actions, having done this preliminary inspection of your own thought process and actions can spare you a lot of possible problems and irritating social interactions coming from other people. After all, if someone was blaming you for a mistake that they themselves had made, you most likely would not be in the greatest of moods, so it is only normal to expect the same behavior from others.

In addition to helping you find the source and the solution to your situation, questioning your own thought process and actions before venturing into anything else will often help you get a clearer picture of the situation as a whole, and can help you guide others to figure out where the problem stems from. You can start by asking others the very same questions you just asked yourself. Having just analyzed every part of your own processes, you most likely have a good idea of what is relevant to the situation at hand and what is not. Knowing what is relevant or not is incredibly helpful when you are at the point where you have to filter through your peers' dialogue in order to find clues, explanations or solutions. Here's an example: let's say there is an issue, and you have already narrowed down the number of possible sources from which it might come by analyzing the situation on your own. When you then question a friend or a colleague about this issue, you can probably dismiss the parts where he or she is considering one of the paths you've already crossed out, and mention your own analysis in order to focus your energy on the most likely suspects. However, as always, it is possible that you might have overlooked something in your own analysis, so you shouldn't dismiss everything right away without first lending an ear and entertaining the thought again for a moment, just to see if a new idea might be triggered by the other person's words.

Furthermore, having inspected every detail of your own thoughts and actions will likely prove crucial to clear and efficient communications once you start questioning and looking for answers with others. As I have mentioned previously, it is common behavior for most to lash back when questioned on their actions, especially when you are looking for the source of an issue. Therefore, it is possible that the people you talk with will start questioning you in return, before they even start to question themselves. Your initial reflection on your own processes will help you provide clear answers to others' questions, as your own doings and reflections in the situation will be fresh in your memory and well thought out. Your understanding and analysis of the situation will also be better than it previously was, so you will be able to explain things more precisely to others, and to better grasp the essence and the value of their response.

In such cases where you have questioned yourself and then questioned others only to be questioned back by them, do not despair. Your own analysis of the situation should allow you to more easily inform others by providing them with clear and simple answers to their interrogations, while you remain calm and open-minded when time comes for them to respond again.

Staying open-minded

It is important to keep in mind that even after a deep reflection on everything you have done, it is still possible that you have missed an element that will prove instrumental in solving your problem. It is, after all, the very basis of this principle that you are capable of making mistakes and that you should be intrinsically aware of that fact. This is why it is important to remain open minded in your discussions with others when attempting to find a solution.

At any point, someone might ask you a question that you did not think about. It is also possible that at some point, someone's words or actions will act as a trigger in your brain and unlock a train of thought that you had not previously entertained. When that happens, you should once again begin by questioning yourself and analyzing your own actions before moving on to others. Applying the principle at every thought level is the only way to truly take advantage of all the benefits it can bring you.

Now, there is a lot more to be said about this, so I will be going a little more in depth on the subject throughout this book. If you just cannot wait, feel free to jump to the *An example about social interactions* section of the next chapter for an explanation on how this can improve your relationships with friends, family, coworkers and even strangers. You can then come back to this page... or jump to another section! It's your book, after all: it's up to you to decide how you experience it.

Obviously, there are also drawbacks to applying this mindset in your everyday life. We will touch on those in a later chapter. For now, let me give you a few examples of this mindset being applied in real life situations.

Chapter 2

Real Life Examples

The following examples are sourced from my own experience. Parts of those stories and examples are redacted or generalized for the sake of simplicity and clarity, but you will find that all of the relevant information has been kept in. By writing and sharing this chapter, my objective is to help you understand how this mindset can help you improve your everyday life. To do so, I will tell you about a few of the ways in which it helps me in my own life. In short, this chapter should allow you to piece together how the theory behind this book can be applied in the real world.

I will present three distinct scenarios in this chapter. Although they are all set in different parts of life, you will find that they are fairly similar once you look at them with this book's basic principle in mind. The first scenario is programming-related, which is only natural as it is the activity that lead to my "discovery" of this mindset. The second scenario relates to education, and helps to explain how this principle can prove helpful when learning new things. The third and final scenario takes place within the context of a social interaction, and serves as an example of how the mindset can be used in your everyday interactions with people. Now, let us get started.

An example about programming

This first example will be slightly more technical: it describes a real-life scenario that happened to me fairly frequently when debugging or trying to better understand a snippet of code. If you don't know much about programming, or even computers in general, you shouldn't worry: I will explain everything in layman's terms to ensure that we are all on the same level. I wrote this section not because you need to learn more about how programming works, but because I feel that this example is essential to the understanding of where the base principle came from. So, without further ado, let's dive into the thought processes that this mindset was derived from.

When you are working as a developer, whether you are building a website, a mobile app, or an extraordinarily complex and optimized program to launch rockets into space, you spend a lot of time thinking and analyzing the task at hand. You try to figure out what the simplest solution that covers all of your bases might be. Then, you think about it some more in order to find flaws and scenarios in which that solution might not work as expected. If you find any, you think some more about those flaws and how you might be able to alter the initial solution in order to improve it; to make it bulletproof. Once that bit of mental gymnastics is done, you prepare to do a few more flips and splits in your head as you try to figure out how that solution can be implemented within the scope and limitations of your project. It is only once you are done with all of those reflections that you start writing code.

This initial process can take anywhere between a few seconds to a couple of weeks or months, depending on the scale and complexity of the task. Now, with all of those thoughts, analysis and preparations, you might expect the development itself to go down smoothly. After all, you have thought about every possible scenario and found solutions to every flaw ahead of time: what could possibly go wrong?

Well, as it turns out, there are many things that can go wrong. Some problems are easy to detect:

- you mistyped the name of something;
- your machine does not have enough storage space;

- you don't have permission to access a file

In such cases, a clear error message will be displayed to you. Such messages are usually written in plain English, and include useful information such as the location of the line of code that is at fault. This type of error occurs fairly often - especially the first one - but thanks to the error messages, they are fairly easy to find and fix.

However, there are some issues that can be much more troublesome for a developer:

- a task crashes without any real indicator of what went wrong;
- a task takes much longer to complete than what was expected;
- a third-party library[1] or API[2] does not work as expected

---

[1] A library is a bit of pre-written code that is usually shared and used in multiple projects.

[2] An API, or *application programming interface*, is a way for a program to allow others to use its data and functionalities easily. For example, Google provides APIs which allow developers to embed maps in their

- something works correctly when you do it, but doesn't work when your client does it

As a developer, you end up facing every single one of those issues at one point or another. When that happens, you have to put yourself in a different headspace than when you are simply writing code. You are not creating anymore: you are debugging. If you are not a programmer, the differences between writing code and debugging might not be as obvious to you, but let me illustrate both activities to help you see how they contrast with one another.

When you are writing code or developing something new, you have a specific objective, you most often have a pretty good idea of what the steps to get to that objective are. Your job is then to transform those steps into something that a computer can understand and process. That's basically what code is: instructions that computers can follow and process to do exactly what you ask them to. You can think of it as writing down a recipe you already know and love... with the small exception that you have to

---

programs, to get information about a business's location, to generate itineraries between locations, etc.

make your instructions so simple and yet specific that even a 3-year-old could do it if he followed them to a T. Contrary to popular belief, computers are not very smart, they're just really good at doing what you ask them to do really quickly. So, sometimes, to get the computer to do what you want it to do, you have to get creative. But I digress... In summary, when you are writing code, you have a set objective and you usually know how to achieve it, so you often just have to turn your thoughts into code, and *voilà*! A new feature is born.

When you are debugging, it's quite different. Of course, you have an objective as well: your goal is to fix the issue at hand. Oftentimes, you have a good idea of where the issue might lie. Other times, you have no clue whatsoever, and you have to analyze and research every bit of code you stumble on in order to understand what's happening. You can think of it like solving an old jigsaw puzzle without the picture on the box. Sure, you might have a rough idea of which colors and shapes you are looking for, but there's thousands of pieces to look through, so it could take a while. Wait, what is that? That piece is not even part of this puzzle! And why does it feel like there's pieces missing?

Well, there's always a chance that you'll get lucky and find the piece you need right away, but either way, the point is as follows: debugging can be fun, but it can also be infuriating. You know your end goal, just like when writing new code, but there's a lot of unknowns between you and that goal. It's a tedious process that can take a lot of time and analysis, and it's everything but straightforward. That is why I think it's important to mention that debugging requires you to be in a completely different headspace then when you are developing new things.

Now, let's get back to our original subject matter. In this example, the type of issue I will be talking about is the following: something works when you do it, but not when your client does it. I use this type of issue as an example because I believe it is the easiest one to understand, whether you have any technical knowledge or not. So, let's dig in.

In my earlier days as a developer, I developed a small piece of software that allowed my client to easily create designs for funeral bookmarks and other items of the sort. It was a simple program that didn't require any complicated installation or setup process: I just gave the client a USB memory stick with a folder inside, which contained the program and a few other files it needed to run, and that was it. All the client had to do was to drag that folder on his desktop, and he could run the program that was inside.

At one point, after I had added a new feature to the program and sent him the updated version, the client told me that the program didn't work correctly anymore. Functionalities that had been working previously had now stopped working, and crashed the program whenever you attempted to use them. However, on my computer, the program worked flawlessly. I was using the exact same version that my client was using, and I had installed it exactly as he had done, yet it worked on my computer and not on his.

Now, I knew my client was not very tech-savvy. He had had issues in the past when installing the program, so that lead me to believe that he just made that same type of mistake again. I started asking him a bunch of questions about how he did it, but everything seemed fine. After a while, it started to feel like he was getting frustrated with this issue, and so was I. I was so sure that he had simply done something wrong that I couldn't figure out what should have been obvious to me as a developer.

As it turns out, the new version of the program that I had sent him required a new library[3] in order to run correctly. Now, I already had that library file on my computer because of a previous project, but I had forgotten to add it to the package that I sent my client. So, whenever he tried to use the new feature, the program went looking for that file but never found it as it wasn't available on his computer, so the program crashed.

Obviously, this was a fairly simple problem to solve for me once the cause was found: all I had to do to fix the issue was to add the missing library file in the program's folder, as I had done for other libraries before. What matters in this story is not the simplicity of the solution. After all, the solutions to most of the issues we face in life are much simpler than the issues themselves. No, what really matters in this story is the way that I went about figuring out what was wrong. I made assumptions based on my previous experiences with my client, and I tried to validate those

---

[3] For non-technical folks, a library in the software development world usually comes in the form of a file that people already have on their computer, or that comes with a piece of software.

right away, thinking that a mistake on their end was causing the issue. Now, however probable it might have been, going to them right away with this assumption was a mistake.

What I should have done instead is… yes, you guessed it: I should have assumed I was wrong; that I was the one at fault. With that basic assumption in mind, I would have taken more time to analyze what was happening, breaking the process into smaller steps. That would have allowed me to figure out which part of the process was problematic, and from that I would most likely have been able to pinpoint my error.

As dumb and simple as that might sound, it can be very difficult to take a step back from your initial reaction. After all, that makes a lot of sense: most often than not, your gut feeling will indeed be right. However, it's that one in fifteen[4] times where it is wrong that can really be damaging. In this example, it made my client feel bad as I

---

[4] Feel free to adjust this statistic based on your own error rate in life. Mine ranges anywhere between 1/200 and 1/2, mostly depending on how focused I am… and also on whether I had to skip breakfast or not.

was basically accusing him of messing up (in a polite way, of course), and it made both of us waste valuable time for no good reason.

Nowadays, when I when receive an email or a phone call from a client telling me that something doesn't work, I never try to give them an answer right away - even if that client has come to me with the same issue every week for the past two months and they were the one at fault every time. I always take the extra time to analyze the situation, see if we've made any changes recently that could have caused this, if our servers might be having some issues at the moment, or if we have any logs that indicate that there is an error in my code. If, after all of that initial research, the issue really seems to be coming from them, I will always try to find conclusive evidence of their mistake, as well as a solution to fix it, before I reach out to them to inform them. If no conclusive evidence of a mistake on their end can be found, please don't start throwing the blame around: it won't do anyone any good. Simply go back to the drawing board and do some more tests and research.

Maybe a friend or a colleague has experienced a similar thing before and found a solution. Or maybe a stranger has, and he just so happened to write about it in a blog article or on a forum. Maybe the problem you're facing is just a symptom of a larger problem, and that's what you should be looking to fix. Try to look at things from a different angle: changing your point of view can often help bring new ideas. Sometimes, that will lead you exactly where you needed to end up. Other times, it won't do much. Even if you don't get the results you were hoping for, the mere fact that you're putting in the effort shows that you care, and that matters a lot.

We have a tendency to remember the bad things and to overlook the good ones – or even worse: to let the bad things taint the good ones. So, you should make a bit more effort in every situation to avoid starting or participating in the blame game. It's a game that nobody likes, and it rarely leads to the resolution of the issue at hand.

An example about education

In today's world, people often spend the first two decades of their life in schools, educating themselves on a variety of topics. Now, whether you like the way the system is set up or not, it's undeniable that education is a very important part of all of our lives. We start learning from the first day of our life, and we learn a little more almost[5] every day until our last. So, with that in mind, taking time and energy to learn and apply a mindset that helps you improve the way you educate yourself seems like a reasonable investment, doesn't it? Well, the following example will show you how the "When in doubt, assume you're wrong" mindset can indeed prove itself useful in the field of education.

A lot of people have difficulty in school. Some have issues understanding the concepts that they are being taught. Some have a hard time studying. Some can't seem to remember the theory when comes time for a test or an exam. Each person has their own struggles when it comes to learning new things, remembering them, and applying them in practice.

Most of these struggles come from having a tough time committing new information to memory, and recalling that information when it is required. Now, memory is a

---

[5] Some days we just lay on the couch all day and do absolutely nothing, so we are not really learning anything. I doubt there is anything I can do to help you on those days, so I added "almost" to that sentence to give the both of us a little leeway.

very complex subject matter, and it is not one I can confidently go into detail about; I have not done any neuroscience-related studies and I myself have what I would consider to be a below average memory. However, through my personal experiences, a few Google searches and some of the exchanges that I have had with my mother (who did study neuropsychology for a bit), I have come to a few conclusions that I believe most people will find helpful.

From the learner's point of view, the main objective of education is to take in information, to understand what it means and how it can be put to use, and to commit it to long-term memory. This objective is clearly divided in three steps. Let's dive into each one of those to see how the mindset can help you.

That first step, taking in the information, is almost completely in your teacher's hands, whether he is an actual person standing in front of you, an online course, or a book. There isn't much we can do to help with that one[6].

The second step, understanding the material as well as when and how to use it, is partly in your teacher's hands and partly in yours. If this is where the issue lies for you, you can do some more research on the subject; the Internet can give you almost any information you might need, in any format you might like.

If you keep trying and you still don't understand how something works, you should try to sprinkle in a bit of doubt into the parts you already know. I find that often times, diving back into the pre-requisites or the basic concepts behind something can do one of two things. It can allow me to free my mind of the new information, which gives me a blank slate and makes it easier for me to understand the advanced concepts when I get back to them. Also, it can make me realize that I had misunderstood or missed something in one of the pre-requisites, which was

---

[6] Unless you're absent, distracted or not paying attention. In that case, maybe start by showing up to class, taking off your earbuds, doodling a little less and leaving your phone in your pockets.

making it much more difficult (or impossible) to understand how the advanced concepts can possibly work. You can try to create a great song all you want, but if you aren't tuning your instrument correctly, there's a good chance you won't get the results you were expecting. So, whenever you don't understand something after you try your hardest, go back and take a look at the different steps and pre-requisites that come with it.

The third step is to commit the newly acquired knowledge to long-term memory. This is where the mindset gets really interesting. However, before we talk about that, let's get into the basics of memory, just so we know what we are working with.

There are multiple types of memories. There are explicit memories, which are the memories that you can consciously recall just by thinking about them. There are procedural memories, which is what motor skills and muscle memory are. The most interesting type for us, however, is priming. You know how some words automatically come to mind when you think of another related word? That's part of what priming memory is. The two memories are somehow linked or close to one another in your brain, and when the first one comes up, it acts as a trigger and your brain is much more likely to remember the other memory. For example, when you read, hear or say the word "bacon", you're likely to think about "egg", as the two often come as a pair, "bacon & eggs". If you hear "banana", you might think about the color yellow, or about other fruits such as strawberries. I could give you many more examples, but I think you got the idea.

Now, you might wonder why word and concept associations in your brain mean that this book's mindset can help you study. Well, the idea is simple: first, you try to consciously create such associations when you are studying. You can do so by boiling down entire concepts to simple keywords, by creating stories about them, by associating existing memories to them, etc. Then, when the time for the exam, the test or the presentation comes, you will have an easier time remembering the information. If you do forget something, you can dissect the process or the problem you are facing. By thinking about and analyzing each step, from the most basic to the most complex, it is highly likely that you will either come across a keyword or a concept that will act as a trigger for the desired memory to come back up to the surface, or that the analysis itself will help you figure out what it is you are missing.

Although I have used that process a bit for tests and exams as well, my favorite examples for this are class presentations. Early on in school, whenever I had a presentation to do, I always wrote an entire text beforehand, and practiced that speech until I remembered every single word of it. Then, as you might have already predicted, I would forget entire sections of the text when I got in front of the class, so I would have to stop and look at my text on a sheet of paper, trying to figure out where the heck I was so I could keep the presentation going.

One of my favorite examples of how using pre-written speeches went incredibly wrong for me is the following. Back in high school, I had a presentation to do. In order to make things more interesting, and to get people's attention right away, I decided to make things a little more theatrical, so I wrote my speech with that in mind. My presentation actually started with me standing outside of the classroom, barging in and slamming the classroom door, which was followed by me yelling a military-type order of some sort. Now, that went brilliantly: I got everyone's attention, got some a few people laughing, and I even managed to get a hint of a smile from the teacher. However, things took a turn for the worse when I forgot the rest of my speech just three or four lines later. Oh, and did I mention we weren't allowed a cheat sheet? At that point, what was supposed to be a great theatrical and immersive presentation had suddenly turned into silence and embarrassment. I could not for the life of me remember the rest of my speech, so I ended up having to do the walk of shame back to my desk and letting others do their presentation for the rest of that period. One or two days later, I had to do my presentation again, and as you can imagine, the surprise was kind of ruined that time, and the only laughs I got in that initial part of the presentation were from people who thought I would screw it up again. Needless to say that at that point in my life, I was quite ashamed of that whole experience.

So, at some point after that incredibly embarrassing presentation, I decide to switch things up, as remembering texts never seemed to work as well as expected. What I started doing next was exactly what I described above. I started thinking ahead of time about what I wanted to talk about, and boiled down entire concepts to just one word, which I could then write on my notes or on my slides. The rest was improvisation.

Now, for most people, improvising an entire presentation can be quite scary the first few times, especially if you're used to memorizing texts. However, you can prepare yourself at home before you go in front of the class: simplify the concepts, come up with simple keywords or images that you can remember or write down, and associate the things you want to talk about to those keywords or images. Then, all you have to do is practice! It doesn't matter if your speech or your syntax is perfect or not. By remembering the concepts and information when you need it instead of reciting a speech, you will find yourself being much more engaging for your audience, and conveying the information much more clearly than if you were stuttering your way through a pre-prepared speech. Plus, if you need to fill in more time because your teacher has set specific time limits, you can ramble a little bit more about your subject, maybe even sprinkle in a bit of humor or interaction with your audience if it's appropriate. The opposite is true as well: if you are going on for too long, you can often condense the rest of your presentation. It's much easier to respect time limits when you decide what you say on the fly than if you are reciting a speech, seeing as the latter has a finite number of words and sentences that you are often forced to stick to.

Now, I used presentations as my example, but there are plenty of other scenarios in which using memory priming to your advantage can be achieved, especially in the education realm. Another example would be cheat sheets, and any other type of personal notes, for that matter. Let's say you are allowed half a page of notes for an exam. If you try to cram everything you might be needing in details on there, you're either going to run out of space or write everything so small that you can barely read it when the time comes. Plus, it might be more difficult to find the specific information you're looking for when you need it. However, if you write down only the most complicated concepts, processes and formulas – the ones that simply cannot be remembered – and use keywords and memory triggers for the rest of the information, you will have plenty of space to write own everything you need. Plus, the extra space it will free up might allow you to organize the information in a way that helps you easily find it when you need it.

The important thing is to make sure you're using triggers that work for you, not just keywords you found online or in a textbook. Although they are often similar, everyone's triggers can be different, so what your friend writes down in their notes might not help you remember, and vice-versa. Get creative, experiment, and figure out what works best for you. It might take you some time to get used to in the beginning, but once you figure out what works for you, it will become much more efficient than regular note taking and you won't be able to do it in any other way.

So, in summary: your brain is great at associating memories together, so use that to your advantage and break things down when you need to in order to find the triggers that will allow you to remember the information you need more easily.

Before we are done talking about education, there is one last thing I would like to mention, and it can also be applied to work or any other type of situation in which the results of your work will be judged by others. The basic principle behind the mindset being that you should make sure that you have done everything you can, analyzing your own work and thoughts, before starting to look for flaws in other people's work... please, resist the urge to blame your teacher right away if you get feedback indicating that you did something wrong, such as a bad grade on a test. This also applies to your manager, boss, or whoever validates the quality of your work in your professional life, and to your parents, friends and loved ones in your personal life. Take a minute to think about how you could have done things better, and how you can improve yourself for the next time instead. In some cases, it is possible that you are not the one at fault, but as always, you should accept and correct your own faults before attempting to point out mistakes that others may or may not have done.

An example about social interactions

A lot of people are interested in improving their relationships with the people they interact with in their life, whether they are friends, colleagues, lovers or complete strangers. Well, using the *When in Doubt* mindset and the principles it is based on can actually help you do that if you are willing to put in a little bit of effort to apply them.

Most of us have heard of "the golden rule", or at least some variation of it. It's found in the bible, in Chinese philosophy, and in pretty much every other religion, philosophy and culture there is. The crux of it, in case you are not familiar with it, is to not do to others what you wouldn't like to have them do to you. Now, that's very easy to understand in theory, but putting it in practice is often a lot more difficult. As soon as someone says something that questions what we do, or something that can be considered mildly offensive or blameful towards us, our emotions and our ego get involved and we react almost immediately. We get defensive, finding excuses or blaming someone else, or even worse, we get on the offensive and retort with an attack, pointing out the other person's flaws and problems. This is an incredibly toxic yet natural habit for us humans. We're all wild animals to begin with, so our instinct often pushes us to get into fight or flight mode at the mere sight of confrontation. Overcoming this instinct is one of the most helpful things you can do to improve your relationships.

Now, don't get me wrong: overcoming this and changing the way you react to other people in social interactions might be one of the most difficult things you do; it surely is the most difficult advice to apply in this book. Our interactions are often fast-paced, without much time for reflection and self-interrogation. However, if you do put in the time and effort to change the way you react to people's questions and comments, as we're about to dive into, you'll likely find it's the most important things you'll have gotten out of this book. So, let's get into it.

Even though we have come up with words and sayings to describe just about everything with incredible precision, most of us aren't literate enough to know and confidently use those words to express ourselves perfectly in our everyday conversations. We can also be pretty bad at times in the way our tone or body language align with what we feel when we are talking to others. As you might have already guessed and experienced, those shortcomings often lead to confusion, misunderstandings, and people feeling attacked, especially when we spurt out our initial reactions as a response without any second thoughts. In actuality though, people are usually just trying to convey their thoughts and ideas as best as they can in the given moment.

Now, at the root, the *When in Doubt* mindset is all about slowing down and questioning yourself before taking action, and it's no different when it comes to social interactions. In a nutshell, the idea is to take in what the other person says and to analyze it in order to construct a thoughtful and considerate response, instead of going with whatever comes to mind right away. Making sure you don't respond to other people's genuine feedback and suggestions negatively just because you feel slighted by them is what this is all about.

When someone gives you their opinion on something you did or said, or points out a problem that you might be responsible for, the first step is to bypass your ego. Getting defensive without a reasonable logical explanation won't help you much, and taking everything people say as a personal attack on you is certain to get you absolutely nowhere. Deconstructing what they said and taking time to find solutions and logical explanations or to acknowledge that what they said was actually honest and constructive criticism will always be better received than tearing apart everything they said, than finding excuses or than getting emotionally triggered for no good reason.

I've said it before and I will say it again: this is not an easy habit to overcome. We have all been in situations where we perceived other people's opinions and reactions much more negatively than they really were. The most common reasons for that are as such:

- Their opinion goes against our own.
- We don't understand why their opinion is as it is.
- Their explanations were unclear or confusing to us.

A good example of a situation that includes all three of these has happened to me quite recently. We were having difficulties with the tools we were using at work, and were looking for alternatives. Seeing as we are a web development agency who just so happens to develop applications for other companies, I, along with a few others, suggested that we build our own tools instead of migrating to another existing tool. My point was that we had already moved from one tool to the other once or twice before, and that it was highly likely that the next tool also wouldn't fit our needs nearly as perfectly as in-house tools could. However, when I presented this idea to a friend and colleague of mine, I didn't feel like he was really open to the idea, and I was kind of bummed out. We had a bit of back and forth every now and then about the subject, but the situation stayed pretty much the same. Then, at some point, he set up a meeting with me and a few other friends and colleagues to try and open up the lines of communication and figure out what we were going to do. In that meeting, he expressed his doubts and his fears, and we took the time to discuss those, and to provide clarifications on what we had in mind. What I then realized was that as it turned out, that friend was on our side as well! What I had initially perceived as a hard "no" was in fact just him having doubts and uncertainties that he needed reassurance with. In the end, I realized that all of that time of awkwardness could have been avoided if I simply took more time to analyze what he was saying and to talk to him about it. We would've both felt much better about it, instead of lingering and carrying this useless weight on our shoulders for weeks.

When you take the time to reflect on what people say and find solutions and meaningful responses instead of focusing on how they said it or how they might have wronged you, people will often appreciate talking with you a lot more. Your conversations are also much more likely to be enjoyable, interesting and productive, as you won't be getting distracted and tripped up by every little slight and miscommunication. This previous example lasted a few weeks and was easily resolved in the end. However, if you aren't attentive to such things and don't make an effort to fix them while they're still fresh, they can build up and turn into lifetime grudges – and no one wants that.

What's more, even those who are intentionally trying to trip you up – which is much rarer than you think, by the way – will often give up on their negative attitude with you if you keeping diffusing the situation by not reacting as they expect. Who knows, they might even follow your lead and change their ways when talking to you. Either way, not giving in to your ego and emotions in those situations can only help.

Now, as you might expect, there is a balance to achieve when you do this. If you take too much time to analyze what others are saying, you might end up overthinking things, or not having time to respond before other people talk or before the subject changes. For some, achieving this balance will be easy. For others, it might be so difficult that applying this mindset turns them into mutes, effectively making things worse than they were originally. If this is your case, know that this issue can be resolved by practicing. Sticking to the mindset in situations and scenarios in which you are more comfortable, whether it's when talking with close friends or with strangers, or when interacting with people via text messages, will help you get used to it and speed up your ability to reflect and react thoughtfully and appropriately over time.

Now, everything that was said so far was about responding to other people's comments. However, that's just half of it. The other half is how you talk to people to begin with; how you express your own comments, feedback and ideas to other people. Luckily for you, it's quite simple: the same basic rules can be applied. Before you talk, just think about what the point you want to get across is, and make sure you say it in a thoughtful way, to try and avoid putting other people in a defensive position. That's all there is to it!

So, just in case you needed a more concise and slightly more direct explanation to remember what we just talked about, here it is: before you say something, make sure there's value in what you are saying, and that you are conveying your ideas thoughtfully. Otherwise, you're likely just shitting on other people's work and ideas without any real purpose.

After all, there is a good reason why the golden rule is present in just about every philosophy there is: it's just the right thing to do.

Chapter 3

The Drawbacks

If you have read every word of this book up to this point, it might have dawned on you that the basic principle that is being presented can seem to be a rather grim one. To be fair, it is a fairly negative way of looking at things. Using self-doubt as a tool for personal and professional improvement can be a double-edged sword, so it must be wielded carefully and with proper preparation in order to get the most benefits with as little of the negatives as possible. This is why I thought it essential to include this chapter: in order to present the drawbacks that come with this mindset. Despair not, however, as this chapter will also give you advice on how to avoid those drawbacks, or at the very least minimize their impact.

Stress and self-doubt

Let's begin with one of the most major issues that you will inevitably end up facing at one point or another, whether you chose to apply this mindset to your everyday life or not. At some point, you will feel stressed that you might have made a mistake, or that you aren't good enough to do something. Although this already happens to everyone, if you are not careful, it can happen to you much more often once you start applying this mindset. After all, stress often comes from self-doubt to begin with, so it's only normal that using self-doubt as a tool in most of your reflections may lead to more stress.

The solution to that drawback comes in two parts. The first part is simple: you have to realize that by introducing doubt in the process early on, you have most likely reduced the likelihood of errors by quite a bit. Applying this mindset to your life will often push you to put safeguards, safety checks and additional verifications in place before any issue has occurred, because you have considered the possibility that you might have made a mistake and that errors might indeed occur. Reminding yourself that you have taken those precautions should allow you to reduce your level of stress in those situations where you start doubting yourself unintentionally. Additionally, the mere fact that you took those additional precautions will likely reduce the frequency of those stressful situations to begin with, so you have less to worry about.

The second part of the solution is actually much simpler to explain than the first. In fact, it is not limited to this mindset, so most of you already know some variation of it. As a wise animal once said: "Hakuna Matata". Just take a step back, and relax. Although it is easier said than done, freeing yourself of your worries is guaranteed to also make you stress-free. Therefore, if you have already taken time to better analyze and taken additional precautions to avoid errors, you should not worry as much afterwards. Of course, some worry can still be good for you, as it might help you avoid more problems that you hadn't yet thought about. To figure out what you should and should not be worrying about is very easy. In fact, most of the literature about stress and worry can be boiled down to this one simple guideline: if you can't fix something, don't worry about it. This guideline on its own might even be of more use to you than the mindset this entire book is based on, so whether or not you decide to apply the mindset to you every life, please remember this one guideline.

On the same line of thought, I also think it's important to mention that although it might not seem so, everyone doubts themselves and feels a bit incompetent at times. The impostor syndrome is very real, especially in a world where everyone broadcasts their successes but not their failures. It is completely normal to doubt your decisions and your accomplishments, and to feel like at some point someone will raise the curtain and expose you as a fraud. When it does happen, try to remind yourself that every other person out there has felt the same way, even the most successful people you can think of. You got where you are for a reason. You are not a fraud. Don't let doubt hold you back: cage it and use it as a tool for self-improvement.

Instead of fearing situations in which you are scared and doubting yourself, chase them. Situations that scare the shit out of you are extremely helpful and formative in the long run, and it's the kind of thing that allows you to grow. So, don't be afraid to start that personal project, or to take a trip to a country with a different culture and language, or to quit that job that doesn't satisfy you. You never know what might happen if you make the move... unless you try it. And really, what do you have to lose?

The fact that you are reading this book is a great example of what can result from applying that exact piece of advice. When I started working on this book, I was scared shitless of how it would be received, and of what people might think of me when the time would come for me to announce that I wrote a book. In fact, I am still unsure of what the peoples' reaction will be as I am writing this. But here's the one thing I do know: if I publish this book and no one reads it or likes it, I will be sad for a bit, and then I will move on to something else, be happy I tried and forget about it. If I let self-doubt guide that decision and give up, I know for a fact that I will resent myself forever for not having done it. I will never know if it could have reached and helped people or not. In the end, I would much rather end up being a happy old man who smiles and laughs about all of the things he's tried than one who spends his time wondering what he could have been if only he had given it a shot. Regret is a poison, but finding the courage to face your fears and do the things that scare you the most is the cure.

Delays

Another issue that ensues from the "when in doubt, assume you're wrong" principle is that it requires you to slow down and think a bit more than what you would usually do. Therefore, it often takes slightly more time to arrive at your final conclusion than if you had just trusted your initial gut feeling and ran with it. Most times, the time difference is negligible: taking a few more seconds or minutes to analyze and verify things won't affect your schedule. However, there will be occasions where taking the time to follow your thought process to the end and validate it at every step along the way will end up taking anywhere from half an hour to an entire day, and possibly even more.

Sadly, there are no quick and simple solutions for this. Still, there is a positive aspect to this drawback. When you take the time to think about every step in whichever process it is you're going through, you will often find other issues that you weren't looking for in the first place, and paying attention to those issues instead of brushing them off can allow you to improve the process, or to overhaul or replace it completely. Over time, as you think about the things you do in your everyday life, doing this should help improve just about every single one them, from cleaning dishes to managing your personal relations, and everything in between.

And here's the best part: you won't be the only one benefiting from this! In the long run, both you and the other people you interact with will be happier that you took the time to reflect and ponder instead of giving them a half-assed answer. The last thing you say is almost always the jumping point for the next thing that will be said, so introducing ideas that aren't well thought out can be a very slippery slope to go down if neither you or the other person has the knowledge to correct the mistakes that are made along the way.

For example, if you were to respond to a colleague's question about a project without really taking enough time to think about it, you could lead him down the wrong path, and he won't have a clue until you realize you messed up or someone else does. If that realization comes just a few minutes later, it might not be a big deal. However, if you only come to your senses an hour later and the work has already been done, then the consequences could be quite disastrous. It could cost your company and your clients a lot of time and money to fix, or even worse: it could lead to a client losing trust in you. This is why it's extremely important to allow those moments of pondering, even if they do introduce additional delays.

People might not notice the advantages that comes with those delays right away, but they will end up appreciating that in you; the fact that you always approach problems, questions and decisions with care and thoughtfulness. And I think we can all agree that those are great things to be known for: care and thoughtfulness.

Relationships

While we are on the subject, there are many drawbacks that appear when using this mindset in the scope of a relationship. As we have all been told many times by friends, family, movies, podcasts and every other type of medium there is, good communication is key in relationships. Now this might come as a surprise to you, but introducing doubt in every single thought you have about your relationship is probably not the best way to ensure good communications with your significant other. Although it can work well with some people, most of the time, your gut feeling should be trusted and vocalized. After all, relationships are all about the emotions and feelings of you and your partner, so this is one area in which letting them guide you makes a lot more sense. Still, the mindset can be used to help you describe those feelings and the thoughts that go along with them, as you should always try to avoid laying blame on someone else unless absolutely necessary. So, whenever there is an issue, you should do your best to describe how it makes you feel and how it affects you, instead of targeting the other person and their actions directly.

Another relationship-related drawback that comes with this mindset is that introducing doubt in your reflections might prevent you from realizing that someone likes you. Although that might sound like a small issue that is not worth bringing up, it is an issue that can have a big impact on your life when it does happen, as it can stop potential relationships even before they begin. So, once again, I would advise you to trust your feelings a little more in this area of life. You can keep applying the mindset as well, but do not let it guide you completely.

Dealing with other drawbacks

In the end, there are many issues that ensue from using this mindset to help you in your everyday life. It is not a perfect. You will certainly end up running into many more problems and drawbacks than the ones that I have listed in this book. In most cases, they can be resolved by simply applying the mindset once more, or by doing the exact opposite and ignoring the mindset, trusting your feelings instead. The solution depends on the situation, just like everything else in life. The most important thing to remember is that this is not a science or an absolute. This is a basic idea to try to help you improve your thought processes and communications. So, if you do decide to apply it, be flexible with it. Adapt it to fit your own needs, and be kind to yourself if you make mistakes: you will get better over time.

Chapter 4

A Few More Tips

Over the last few pages, we have covered many concepts and ideas that you can use to improve almost every aspect of your life, provided you put in a little time and effort. If you have been paying attention, you now know that self-doubt can be turned into an invaluable tool to help better yourself. You have also learned about the importance of setting your ego aside in everyday conversations, and about how you can make use of memory priming to learn new things more easily. Hell, if you were *really* paying attention, you might even have learned a thing or two about programming!

At this point, I could ramble on for many more pages, but you have learned the essentials already, and I trust that you will discover many more helpful approaches and theories as you implement this mindset in your own life. Don't be afraid to break it down and adjust it to fit your needs: I handed you a template, now go out there and make it your own. Put things into practice, see what works for you. And please, let me know how it goes: I would love to hear from you.

Now, to finish things off, I still have a few thoughts and good practices that I would like to share with you. Some of them are in the same line of thought as this mindset while others are completely unrelated, but these are a few tips, tricks, habits, ideas and other practical advice that I felt like sharing with my readers. Enjoy!

1. Any task can be accomplished once it's broken down into small enough steps.

2. It's okay to be disappointed. It's okay to be sad. It's okay to be tired. It's okay to cry. Take some time to rest and take care of yourself.

3. Don't compare yourself to others. Compare yourself to your yesterday-self. After a while, you'll find yourself facing a much fiercer enemy, and fighting a much more constructive battle.

4. Don't obsess with finite goals, like buying a house or a car. They become empty and irrelevant from the moment you reach them. Instead, find your core values, and try your best every day to align everything you do with those values. The fulfilment your values provide is infinite.

5. When you're done reading a book, give it to a friend, a family member, a local charity, library or thrift store. Books prefer hands and eyes to bookshelves, so make sure they don't get bored.

6. Knowledge you don't act on is like not having the knowledge at all.

7. Motivation is not the source of action: it's the result of action. It's a chain reaction. If you're not feeling motivated, get started with the smallest task you can find. That will get the ball rolling.

8. Make sure you go outside at least once a day, even if it's just for a few minutes.

9. Don't worry about things that are out of your control.

10. Hug people.

11. Hot tea goes great with ice cream.

12. If you can't stop thinking about something, write it down. It will help clear your mind.

13. There is no shame in going to bed early, especially if you are satisfied with how you spent your day.

14. If you love someone, take the time to go and see them. You never know when they might go. That applies to artists you like, too.

15. The best way to learn how to do something is to jump right in and do it.

16. If you want to get a shy person talking, find out what their passions are and ask them about those.

17. If you want a new habit to stick, never go two days without doing it.[7]

18. Music has the ability the change your mood: use that to your advantage.

19. Always try to end discussions on a funny or positive note.

20. Don't be afraid to try new things. Yes, some people will judge you, but they are going to judge you whether you do it or not, so you might as well have done a thing and be happy with yourself.

21. Most fears are irrational, so you shouldn't let them control your life.[8]

---

[7] For more information, look up Matt D'Avella's Two Day Rule.

[8] As a kid, I was scared of mustard. More specifically, of my brother running towards me with a bottle of mustard. Imagine if I had let that fear control my life... what a weird life I would be leading.

Acknowledgments

Many thanks to those who helped me bring this project to life.

In particular, I would like to say thank you to my lovely girlfriend, Catarina, for giving me honest feedback on the book from the initial drafts to the final version. This book wouldn't be half of what it is has become if it hadn't been for you help.

I would also like to say thanks to my friend Kim for designing the cover of this book. What Catarina has done for the interior of this book, you have done for the exterior.

Finally, thanks to you, the reader, for joining me in this journey. I hope you learned something from this book and that it will help you in your own projects.

Printed in Poland
by Amazon Fulfillment
Poland Sp. z o.o., Wrocław

61791708R00038